DR. ASH PACHAURI, PhD
&
DR. SAROJ PACHAURI, MD, PhD, DPH

Simple Steps to Sustainability

A Workbook to Guide Individual Climate Action

Contents

1

Introduction

S imple Steps to Sustainability: A Workbook to Guide Individual Climate Action

Introduction

This workbook is designed to help individuals take practical steps toward addressing climate change and promoting sustainability in their daily lives and communities. Each chapter corresponds to a key theme explored in the main book, **"Small Steps, Big Impact: A Simple Guide to Individual Action and Collective Impact to Tackle Climate Change."** Use this workbook to track your progress, set goals, and reflect on your journey toward positively impacting the environment.

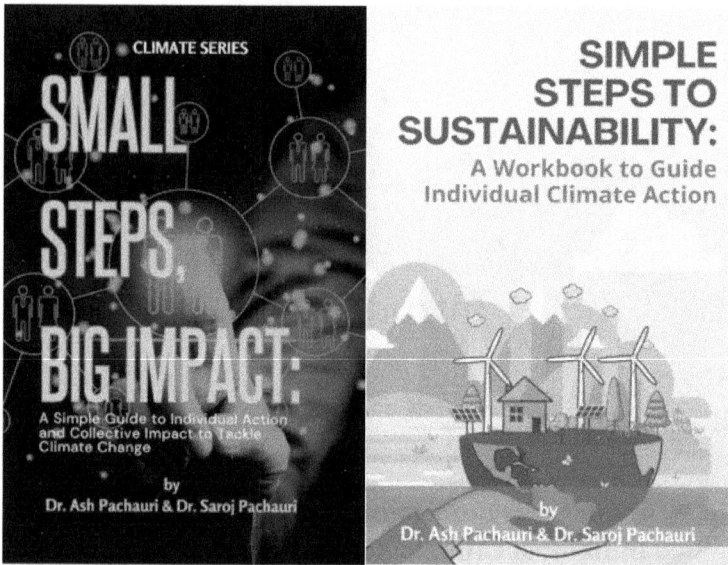

Make small changes in your daily routine to create a big impact on the climate

Key Features

Interactive Exercises: Engage with thought-provoking activities that help you understand the science of climate change, calculate your carbon footprint, and set realistic goals for reducing your environmental impact.

Practical Strategies: Discover actionable steps to enhance energy efficiency, adopt sustainable consumption habits, and make eco-friendly dietary choices.

Community Engagement: Learn how to advocate for climate action, organize community events, and participate in collective efforts to create a more sustainable world.

Personal and Community Resilience: Develop plans to build resilience against climate impacts for yourself and your community, ensuring long-term sustainability and preparedness.

Reflection and Goal Setting: Reflect on your journey, track your progress, and set achievable goals that align with your commitment to environmental action.

Who Is This Workbook For?

This workbook is ideal for all responsible citizens of our planet who want to take action against climate change. Whether you are a student, educator, community leader, activist, or concerned citizen, this workbook offers valuable insights and resources to help you make a positive difference.

What You Will Gain

- A better understanding of climate change and its global and local impacts.
- Practical tools to reduce your carbon footprint and promote sustainability in your daily life.
- Strategies for engaging in effective advocacy and community action.
- Enhanced resilience to climate-related challenges, ensuring a sustainable future for you and your community.
- A sense of empowerment and motivation to continue your climate action journey.

Join the Movement

Using "Simple Steps to Sustainability: A Workbook to Guide Individual Climate Action," you are taking a crucial step towards building a more sustainable and resilient future for yourself and your community. Together, we can significantly impact the climate crisis. Let's take action and build a better world for ourselves and future generations!

2

Understanding Climate Change

A ctivity 1: Research and Reflect

1. Research the basic science of climate change. Summarize what you learned in your own words.

- What are the primary causes of climate change?
- What are the significant impacts of climate change on the environment, biodiversity, and ecosystems?
- What are the impacts of climate change you have experienced? How do they make you feel (anxious, angry, helpless)? What can you do to tackle the impacts of climate change as you experience them?

Reflection

Write a short reflection on how understanding the science of climate change has influenced your perspective on the issue.

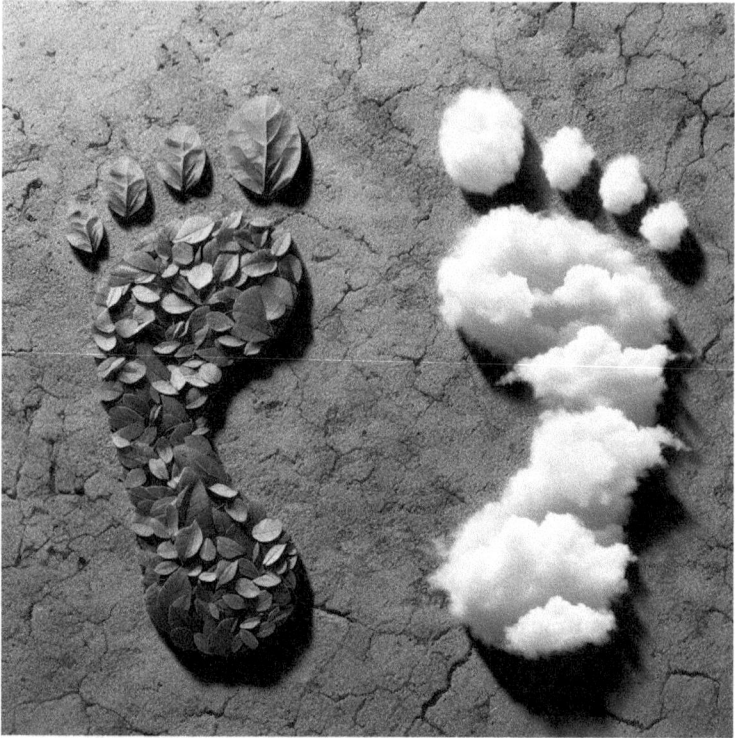

What steps can you take to lower your carbon footprint?

Activity 2: Personal Carbon Footprint Calculation

1. Use an online carbon footprint calculator to estimate your carbon footprint.

- What are the primary sources of your carbon emissions?
- What surprised you about your carbon footprint?

UNDERSTANDING CLIMATE CHANGE

Reflection

Identify three areas where you can reduce your carbon footprint. List specific actions you will take in these areas.

7

3

Energy Efficiency

Activity 1: Home Energy Audit

1. Conduct a basic energy audit of your home.

- Identify areas where you can achieve greater energy efficiency (e.g., insulation, lighting, appliances).
- Create a checklist of energy-saving actions you can implement.

Reflection

What changes will you make to reduce energy consumption in your home? How will these changes impact your carbon footprint?

Opt for renewable energy sources

Activity 2: Renewable Energy Options

1. Research renewable energy options available in your area.

- What types of renewable energy are most accessible to you (e.g., solar, wind, geothermal)?
- What are the potential costs and benefits of switching to renewable energy sources within your home and living

space?

Reflection

What steps can you take to transition to renewable energy sources? Are there any barriers you need to overcome?

4

Reducing Carbon Footprint

Activity 1: Sustainable Transportation

1. Track your transportation habits for one week.

- How often do you use a car, bike, public transportation, or walk?
  - Calculate the carbon emissions associated with your transportation choices.

Reflection

What changes can you make to reduce your transportation-related carbon emissions? Set a goal for incorporating more sustainable transportation methods into your routine.

Choose clean and green transportation to lower your carbon emissions

Activity 2: Dietary Choices

1. Keep a food diary for one week, noting the types of food you consume.

- How often do you eat meat, dairy, plant-based foods, and locally sourced products?

- Research the carbon footprint of different foods.

Reflection

Identify three dietary changes you can make to reduce your carbon footprint. How will these changes benefit the environment?

Your dietary choices affect your health and the health of our planet

5

Sustainable Consumption

Activity 1: Eco-Labels and Certifications

1. Research common eco-labels and certifications for sustainable products (e.g., Fair Trade, USDA Organic).

- Choose a product you regularly purchase and find a sustainable alternative.
- Compare the environmental impact of the two products.

Reflection

How can you incorporate more eco-friendly products into your shopping habits? What criteria will you use to make more sustainable choices?

Activity 2: Waste Reduction Plan

1. Conduct a waste audit of your household.

- Categorize your waste (e.g., recyclables, compostable, land-fill).
- Identify areas where you can refuse, reduce, reuse, and recycle more effectively.

Reflection

Develop a waste reduction plan for your household. What steps will you take to minimize waste and increase recycling?

Minimize waste and ensure proper disposal methods

6

Advocacy and Community Engagement

Activity 1: Write to Your Elected Officials

1. Draft a letter or email to your local or national elected officials.

- Express your concerns about climate change and suggest specific actions they can take.
- Use facts and personal stories to make your case.

Reflection

How can you stay engaged with your elected officials and continue advocating climate action? What other advocacy methods can you explore?

Activity 2: Organize a Community Event

1. Plan a community event focused on climate action (e.g., a clean-up day or educational workshop).

- Outline the goals, activities, and logistics of the event.
- Identify potential partners and resources needed.

Reflection

What impact do you hope to achieve with your event? How can you encourage more people to get involved in climate action in your community?

Rally your peers and community to take climate action

7

Investing in the Future

Activity 1: Sustainable Investment Research

1. Research sustainable investment options such as green bonds or sustainable impact investing.

- Choose one investment option and analyze its potential environmental and financial benefits.
- Consider how this investment aligns with your values.

Reflection

How can you align your financial investments with your sustainability goals? How can you encourage others to consider sustainable investing?

Support, engage with, and invest in green businesses

Activity 2: Support Local Green Businesses

1. Identify local businesses that prioritize sustainability.

- Visit or contact these businesses to learn more about their practices.
- Choose one business to support and reflect on why you chose them.

Reflection

How can supporting green businesses contribute to a more sustainable local economy? How can you support sustainability through your spending habits and consumption choices?

8

Education and Awareness

Activity 1: Create Educational Content

1. Develop educational content about climate change (e.g., a blog post, video, infographic).

- Choose a specific area or impact of climate change to focus on.
- Research and present the information in an engaging and accessible way to share with your friends, family, and community (e.g., via social media or a website).

Reflection

How can you use your skills, accessible media, and platforms to raise awareness about climate change? What impact do you hope to achieve with your educational content?

Each of us has a part to play in combating climate change

Activity 2: Host a Workshop or Presentation

1. Plan and host a workshop or presentation on climate change and sustainability (see attached workshop outline, which you may customize to suit your needs and context).

- Identify your audience and customize your content and delivery to their interests and needs.

- Include interactive elements to engage participants.
- Encourage participants to explore climate actions they can take (see attached guide to individual climate action).

Reflection

What did you learn from hosting the workshop or presentation? How can you continue to educate and inspire others to take climate action?

Workshop Outline

Inspiring Climate Action: Practical Steps for Sustainable Living

Overview

"Inspiring Climate Action: Practical Steps for Sustainable Living" is an interactive workshop designed to provide participants with the knowledge, tools, and inspiration to take meaningful action against climate change. This workshop combines educational content, practical activities, and collaborative discussions to help individuals understand the impact of their choices and empower them to contribute to a more sustainable future.

Objectives

- Educate participants on the science and impacts of climate change.
- Provide practical strategies for reducing personal and community carbon footprints.
- Foster a sense of community and collective action among participants.
- Empower individuals to advocate for policy changes and engage in climate advocacy.

Agenda

1. Introduction and Icebreaker (15 minutes)

- Welcome and introduction to the workshop.
- Icebreaker activity to encourage participant interaction and engagement.

2. Understanding Climate Change (30 minutes)

- Presentation on the science of climate change, its causes, and effects.
- Discussion on the global and local impacts of climate change.

3. Reducing Your Carbon Footprint (45 minutes)

- Interactive session on practical ways to reduce carbon emissions in daily life, including energy efficiency, sustainable transportation, and waste reduction.
- Activity: Personal carbon footprint calculation and goal-

24

setting.

4. Sustainable Consumption and Dietary Choices (30 minutes)

- Presentation on the environmental impact of consumer choices and food consumption.
- Activity: Identify sustainable products and plan eco-friendly meals.

5. Advocacy and Community Engagement (45 minutes)

- Discussion on the importance of advocacy and collective action.
- Activity: Draft letters to elected officials and plan community events.

6. Building Resilience (30 minutes)

- Presentation on personal and community resilience to climate impacts.
- Activity: Creating personal and community resilience plans.

7. Group Activity: Organizing a Climate Action Campaign (45 minutes)

- Collaborative exercise to plan a climate action campaign.
- Participants will work in groups to outline goals, strategies, and action steps.

8. Reflection and Next Steps (30 minutes)

- Participants share their reflections on the workshop and personal commitments to climate action.
- Discussion on how to stay engaged and continue making a difference.

9. Q&A and Closing Remarks (15 minutes)

- Open the floor for questions and answers.
- Summary of key takeaways and closing remarks.

Materials to be Provided:

- Workbook: "**Simple Steps to Sustainability: A Workbook to Guide Individual Climate Action.**
- Carbon footprint calculators and tracking sheets.
- List of sustainable products and resources.
- Templates for advocacy letters and community event planning.

Who Should Attend?

This workshop is ideal for individuals passionate about tackling climate change, including students, educators, community leaders, activists, and anyone looking to impact the environment positively. No prior knowledge is required; it is just a willingness to learn and take action.

Outcomes

By the end of the workshop, participants will:

- Have a strong understanding of climate change and its impacts.
- Understand practical strategies to reduce their carbon footprint and promote sustainability.
- Feel empowered to engage in climate advocacy and community action.
- Have created actionable plans for personal and community resilience.

Join us for this transformative workshop and become a part of the solution to climate change. Together, we can make a difference!

Climate Change: What Can I Do?

Practical Climate Actions

Individuals can significantly impact climate change by adopting various actions in their daily lives.

Here are some practical climate actions one can take:

Reducing Carbon Footprint
1. Transportation

- Use public transportation, bike, or walk instead of driving.

- Carpool or use ride-sharing services.
- Opt for electric or hybrid vehicles.
- Limit air travel and choose direct flights when possible.

2. Energy Consumption

- Switch to renewable energy sources for your home, such as solar or wind power.
- Install energy-efficient appliances and light bulbs.
- Use programmable thermostats to reduce energy use.
- Insulate your home to maintain temperature and avoid energy losses due to poor insulation.

3. Diet

- Reduce meat and dairy consumption, especially beef and lamb.
- Eat more plant-based foods and locally sourced produce.
- Avoid food waste by planning meals and using leftovers.

Sustainable Living
4. Waste Reduction

- Recycle and compost waste.
- Avoid single-use plastics; use reusable bags, bottles, and containers.
- Buy products with minimal packaging.

5. Water Conservation

- Install low-flow showerheads and faucets.

- Turn off faucets rather than leaving them running when water is not in use (for example, brushing, shaving, or in the shower).
- Fix leaks promptly.
- Use a water-efficient washing machine and dishwasher.
- Collect and use rainwater for gardening.

Supporting Sustainable Practices
6. Consumer Choices

- Support companies with sustainable and ethical practices.
- Buy second-hand or high-quality, durable products.
- Choose eco-friendly clothing brands.
- Avoid fast fashion.

7. Advocacy and Education

- Educate yourself and others about climate change and sustainability.
- Support and vote for policies and leaders that prioritize climate action.
- Participate in or donate to environmental organizations.
- Advocate for sustainability initiatives in your community.

Natural Resource Management
8. Gardening and Agriculture

- Plant trees and support reforestation projects.
- Grow your food or support local organic farmers.
- Use sustainable gardening practices like composting and xeriscaping.

Technology and Innovation
9. Adopt Green Technologies

- Use energy-efficient electronics.
- Invest in smart home technologies that save energy.
- Support technological innovations aimed at reducing emissions.

By integrating these actions into daily life, individuals can contribute to a collective effort to combat climate change and promote a more sustainable future.

9

Building Resilience

Activity 1: Personal Resilience Plan

1. Assess your resilience to climate-related impacts (e.g., extreme weather, water shortages).

- Identify areas where you can improve your preparedness and adaptability.
- Create a plan to enhance your resilience.

Reflection

How can building personal resilience help you cope with climate change impacts? What steps will you take to implement your resilience plan?

Activity 2: Community Resilience Project

1. Develop a project to enhance community resilience to climate change.

- Identify a specific climate-related risk in your community (e.g., flooding, heatwaves).
- Outline a project that addresses this risk and engages community members.

Reflection

How can you collaborate with others to build community resilience? What resources and partnerships will you need to implement your project successfully?

Enhance your community's climate resilience

10

The Power of Collective Action

Activity 1: Join a Climate Action Group

1. Research local, national, or international climate action groups and organizations.

- Choose one group to join and get involved with their activities.
- Participate in meetings, events, and campaigns.

Reflection

How can being part of a climate action group increase your impact? What have you learned from working with others towards a common goal?

Together, we can tackle climate change

Activity 2: Organize a Collective Action Campaign

1. Plan and organize a campaign to address a specific climate issue.

- Define the campaign's goals, target audience, and critical messages.
- Develop a strategy for outreach, engagement, and action. What do you hope to achieve as a result of the action taken?

Reflection

What challenges did you encounter while organizing the campaign? How can you overcome these challenges and strengthen future collective action efforts? How can you sustain the efforts you have initiated?

Foster community engagement and momentum to urgently tackle climate change

Conclusion

Congratulations on completing the "Individual Climate Action" workbook! Reflect on your journey and the progress you have made. Identify areas where you can continue to grow, take action, and celebrate your contributions to creating a more sustainable and resilient future.

Final Reflection

Write a reflection on your overall experience using this workbook. How has it influenced your understanding of climate change and your role in addressing it? What are your next steps in continuing your climate action journey?

If you found this workbook helpful, we would appreciate it if you left a favorable review on Amazon!

www.ingramcontent.com/pod-product-compliance
Lightning Source LLC
Chambersburg PA
CBHW070032030426
42335CB00017B/2401